ahadada reader I

Alan Halsey

John Byrum

Geraldine Monk

edited by
Jesse Glass

*aha*dada

books

tokyo / toronto

First Edition
Printed and bound in Japan

Ahadada Books gratefully acknowledges the support of the Foreign Languages Department of Meikai University, Shin-Urayasu, Japan, in the production of this book.

editorial addresses:

3158 Bentworth Drive
Burlington, Ontario
Canada L7M-1M2

Meikai University
8 Akemi, Urayasu-shi
Chiba-ken, Japan 279-8550

Visit Ahadada Books website:
www.ahadadabooks.com

Library and Archives Canada Cataloguing in Publication

Ahadada reader I / John Byrum ... [et al.].

Experimental poems.
ISBN 0-9732233-3-2

1. Experimental poetry, English. 2. Experimental poetry, American. 3. English poetry—20th century. 4. American poetry—20th century. I. Byrum, John, 1952-

PN6101.A39 2004   821'.91408   C2004-904006-5

table of contents

alan

halsey

**THE HUNTING OF THE LIZOPARD RESUMED:
EMBLEMS FROM THE SHIP OF FOOLS LOGBOOK**

'Avi-ucipas oe or naviget m iticyram'

lemures, lamiae, etc.
nymphaea, mandrake, etc.
wormwood, rue, etc.
'forgetting the ἀρχή, insomniacs' *etc.*

⌘

Though familiar with the skies
of Anticyra and the age-old recipes
for hellebore pottage Mercurialis
the Younger chose the pickaxe.

⌘

Certain mouths of hell and places
appointed where the ghosts sometimes
talk with the living 'the lava and ashes
on Mt Hekla rose in March 2000 to 13km'

⌘

The death by remedies,
said Dichotomedes,
when to philosophise
in itself would suffice.

⌘

Those dizzy oysters said the lizopard
had eaten their Christmas Roses.
Their magic so politely professed while they passed
an heap of other accidents, etc., talked of metempsychosis.

⌘

St. Nicholas' crew in the storm he's busy calming or would
if (cover they shift they colour they may they) he could.
'Substance or the unthought' which was known
as Dichotomedes' Lighthouse before its ruin.

⌘

Sugared safeguards at the interference fringes.
'Beyond impatient—butterfly again—unidentified species.'
'Opening the gut we found a black-letter bible and sundry
other volumes in folio, Browne, Burton, etc., with a guide to Lethe.'

⌘

—'and what I say is merely
reading' said one merrily
who when counting unicorns
mistook neurons for nuance -

we are turned to Harpies, feastings to words

STC: INITIALS AS STRUCTURE

'The Pixies' Parlour still exists on a low, sandstone ridge, now some fifty yards from the eastern bank of
the River Otter. In 1986 I crawled in and was astonished to discover the initials STC carved at the very
back of the cave. It took me a moment to realise that the sandstone walls are so porous and flaky that
these could not possibly be Coleridge's original graffiti, but some later act of piety. Such carvings and
re-carvings of his initials, ceremoniously repeated by generation after generation of unknown memori-
alists, suddenly seemed to me like a symbol of the essentially cumulative process of biography itself.'
—Richard Holmes

archive

S & library all in
Terwoven with arbitrary arti
Culated initials a

Symbolical language for deep melancholy consuming ini
Tials at once opposite and
Correspondent within me: beauteous

Spectra of
Two initials orange and violet
Circumstances when peculiar initial differences another's

Shadow's object false-colours its de
Tached initials his innumerable
Cypher

S
Transplanted the mere
Carcase of: an electrical multiplicity of rays and far-

Stretched ini
Tials as a
Co-existing echo you had not

Suspected I am so swallowed up in a
Thousand thousand palimpsest initials of fantasti
C analogue & initial

Similitude: Giant Pyramid ini
Tials Gothi
C Alps and Andes of a world destroyed in a gusty inter

Spersed wilderness howling with emp
Tied gnawing initials leagued in
Conspiracy against me: half-embodying initial

S half images within but harmonious phan
Tom initials fits hints & flashes of refle
Cted light & vast initial

S of
Terra In
Cognita known & anticipated only as an Under-

Song by sub
Tler suppressed initials unified by natural
Contingency: kalligraphical ritual trial initials him

Self as a labyrinth of sweet initials with hillsides I begin to
Think that nothing on earth but it
Could have

Saved me mis
Taking perishible initials for distant
Conceptions where Intuition

S alone are adequate: the neu
Tral product when the I of the
Contra-distinguished initial may exist no longer for it

Self but in the omnipresence of all in each initial & since
Then every error I have
Committed othered when initialled part fugitive part exi

S
Tent only in
Conversation no unapt initial of

Self-experience as a pool with surface ini
Tial without wrinkle the quicksilver initials of metaphysics
Compared in calm weather to

Subtle hieroglyphical ini
Tials blue as smoke at one edge or rainbow initials on fast-sailing
Clouds the

Sensation of shattered fragments of penitent initials put inwardly
Together an immense heap supplying the whole sense wanted: a tra
Ckless unknown initial the last of my being a

Somewhat fitter Ins
Trument than unmeaning blank fuga
Cious initials without material re

Siduum the vivid odorous clusters of initials a sort of music I
Tremble to think what
Cruelly initial recollections the words but initials of air.

THOMAS HOCCLEVE

to my mis reule twenty wyntir excesse
I clappid longe to my chinchy herte
that mirour of riot and malencolie
To have of my balades swich plentee
Whan I sholde go hoom to the privee seel
I am contryt that I swymmed in swich nycetee
destitut of confort and poore souffissance
My thank is qweynt for that I axe is due

WILLIAM DUNBAR

that wes in youthe cald dandillie
hes lang done Venus lawis teiche
making into ballat wyse complaine
quill his tome purs so prikillis him
wan-fukkit funling schit wit craw
Dumbar maid maister bot in mows
scapis in France a knycht of the felde
trublit and feblit now and vexit
as syphir fastand in a nuke
with havie thocht and greif
A sempill vicar I can not be
I can bot ballatis breif

SIR EDWARD DYER

bewailing in Broadgate's-hall my daies of care
iff you will verey Frend put on another mynde
no griefe may compare with the excellentest voice
and elegant Poesie of good M. Sidney or M. Dyer
so Wurshippful a man to doo her Majesties service
I have ben to Prag and saw Master Kelley
conuert appropriat bodies into perfect gold

I have none other refuge but stay of Process
our first *Orpheus*
This Jentleman in plaine Termes told me

ISABELLA WHITNEY

benefits I have even from Childhood receaved of you dere frind
though I to writing fall and made these SLIPS
to refresh my gasing eye not havyng of mine owne to discharg
Good Brother Good Sister Good Cosin Your poore Kinsewoman
wyll show you more then I wryt because I love you well

GABRIEL HARVEY

no bones to take the wall of
what good liking Maister Dyer had of youre Satyricall Verses
happiest Inuentor of the English Hexameter
ink-squittering Howliglasse in Newgate
Piers Penniless the Pamfletter says borrows my name

JOHN DAVIES OF HEREFORD

the Wye neere which yet Vntill we meete in
Oxford where I spend some gaining daies
the Master could so easily disguize his Pen
John Davies of the parish of S$^{t.}$ Dunstan in the West
haue no land but Wales Ile defend
this Scumme of an hotch-potch so hamerd my *Braines*
I give my pictur and The Picture of the Plague
in hate with Loue I feele ryot oreabounds all the recompence
An airy-word I Coniur'd as I could herehence

THOMAS NASHE

a little ape in Cambridge I had all their witchcrafts
Cutbert the queller can cracke a score blades in Iambicks

write a packet of bawdye in all sorts of humors or a Paper-monster
I that made a shewe when the plague detained mee in a house of credit
speedily botcht vp in the *Ile of Wight* my collachrimate fancies
pleased to promise more phantasticall paines
I haue Gunpowder tearmes that will commacerate Howliglasse
that spouted incke in my absence at greate Yarmouth post-haste

ELIZABETH CARY

for too chast a Scholler
a small selfe-portraiture
stolen and printed but called in
Excuse too rash a Mistaking

FRANCIS QUARLES

frequent in his devotions and prayers since
A Feast for Wormes is a Song of Mercy
Periphras'd and Wept in Emblemes and Fancies
Hieroglyphicks of the life of Man and Sions
to retain and admit Your Loyall Subject
O Salvator mundi I appeale to *Cæsar*

HENRY MORE

my *innate* Perswasion a sort of Musical *philosophizing* Murmur
a most savoury *Discrimination* the desire *to know That I may know*
almost extinguish'd and rouz'd out of *Epigram*
I fell into a pretty full Poem called *Psychozoia* or *Life of the Soul*
after no Copy but fetch'd from the Nature of the thing it self
God in a *Dialect* I understand fully speaks to me as a *Friend*
in a Sober Sense *Inhabitant* of *Heaven* upon *Earth*
a private Fellow of Christ's College in Cambridge
that *Chymical* Fire *Chrystaliz'd* into a bright Throne

ANNA TRAPNEL

mony my Mother left me I gave for the relief of the Nation
and the Vision which mentions the horns and cattel and Oxen
their faces and heads like men having on either side their heads a horn
Revelations touching the Lord Protector during 12 dayes in a Trance
I saying they were not to question in *Cornwal* what was spoken
at *White-hall* by an inspiration full of wonder *The Cry of a Stone*
a Sea of glasse there chrystal was which none shall hinder from those thrones

MARGARET CAVENDISH, DUCHESS OF NEWCASTLE

twisted each letter to make such toys as I invent myself
totter'd and torn as pencilled shadows that over-love instructed
my husband will so humour the sense and words of the work
The *Poetresses* World in an Ear-Ring I dresse in my best becoming

THOMAS PARNELL

Then it was that Scriblerus
when we used to meet the Dean and Gay with you
remembered every glass in the chop-house and again
in bad scribbling ink had I Homer's pen

THOMAS GRAY

Orosmades reading Virgil O little heart
ungainly
Nihilissimo in my fondnesses
white Melancholy before that fountain beyond expression
the whole matter to have always something going forward
half a dozen Ballads wrote to divert and the Odikle
my more reasonable excuse
a nothing doing nothing inexplicable and satisfied
among the Cathedrals and Catalogues
with interleaved Linnaeus just come from Netteley by that hanging meadow
a Church-yard Poet must travel or walk out in a Friend's own garding
so solitary as such as I am

ELIZABETH CARTER

as many tongues in my head as by correspondent Friendship
inexhausted Absence
it's Transported Echoes would regulate tho' faint the Transcript
it's short determin'd *Mercy*

THOMAS WARTON

Gothic or magic or pensive or mystic as
Oxford bids me or I choose December for that calm Bower
cloisters and quire where the conscious Echo
or breakfast in the Pot-house with tobacco and puns

ROBERT LLOYD

What I or no one writ but my friend Lloyd in his downright Ease
Nature'll run away with to night if he is there in the Fleet

WILLIAM HAYLEY

a poetical dinner I was surprised by
an exclamation I played with some success

CHARLOTTE SMITH

Giddy composing verses she and all her children
the abyss into which if frenzy seized her husband with
awful ideas of force and danger I need not name but
As to the Sonnets you will give him no information
I am so harrassed with Duns and chicane I am writing
a chapter every day (my <u>trade</u>) of another Novel having
the Rhumatism as I usd to do and I expect strange Defeatures
without returning to a scene I do not know I could bear
as I was I beleive circumstanced and sacrificed
as of a different species the shadowy resemblance

A LIFE OF THE AUTHOR OF 'THE PURSUITS OF LITERATURE'

I[a] cannot[b] think[c] that[d] any[e] subject[f] should[g] be[h] disregarded[i]

[a] It is a voice; nothing more. No man has a right to demand either my name or my situation, but I[aa] am no stranger to the moving principle; so says my friend OCTAVIUS, to whose judgment I submit.

[b] I am solicitous for the end alone. I come in the darkness[bb] of the night, though I can often smile and sometimes be pleased by men whom I forbear to name. Two years have passed since I published "The First Part of the Pursuits of Literature" in an hour of unaccountable indifference. Our peasantry now read Gallick jargon and the *Rights of Man* on mountains and moors. A man of a poetical mind, without the incumbrance of a profession or the embarrassment of business, either wanders into futurity or recals the images of other times and other empires in their gigantick admeasurements.

[c] Privacy is my lot. To my adversaries I never will reply. I love no atheist French Bishops, nor unfrocked grammarians in England. I look upon it as a duty to the publick, and to the Commonwealth of Literature; you may chuse, or rather combine the terms, but it will be idle to make any conjecture as to the author. A poet may be a little playful and ("Ardent, though secret, and though serious, gay") wear *his best black suit.*[cc] See more in future notes. All learning has an index, and every science it's abridgment. Mirabeau said true, "Words are things."

[d] Pale and pensive I[dd] make no apology for my *unsought* quotations; there is a darkness *which may be felt.* Is this the language of an enemy? An injudicious friend is worse. I have raised no phantoms of absurdity merely to disperse them, and I particularly dislike *a mixture of languages.* If I am wrong, I must continue so in the secret affliction of my spirit; yet I am sure I have nothing of the wild American or Kensington Gardens in my composition, and I would maintain an established order, to remember it is pleasant to consider the beginning and progress of great events. LITERATURE IS THE GREAT ENGINE *by which* ALL CIVILISED STATES *must ultimately be supported or overthrown.*

[e] There is unity in the design. I have risen in silence and it repairs me to think in this botanising age that I am speaking to the ministers of the crown of Great Britain. The

time for discrimination seems to be come, and *therefore* I have quite a sufficient excuse, or rather a full justification of my allusion, poured forth as a libation from the cup of Achilles (1794). *Read* the preceding note; my principles are strong unto salvation. No imitation is intended of any former poem, and I[ee] have no romantick ideas of virtues without motives. Words upon words! "Mawkish, and thick ... scarce the tropes supplies." I entered into the sanctuary of the Hebrews and heard the voice of their prophet: "Credidi, propter quod locutus sum." The use of metaphor is to illustrate, not to prove; my motive is more visionary.

[f] Still I pause: I never desired to exhaust any subject. I am UNKNOWN, UNBOUGHT, *and shall be* UNALTERED. I speak to the intelligent, but I have read something about *vitæ summa brevis*, &c. &c. I love the regions of the morning, and the light of the sun; Homer[ff] explains it best. Conscience is a monitor which often needs a guide. *Talkers* are preferr'd.

[g] I must now pass from this subject. I pretend not to be "the sole depositary of my own secret". The notes are not always merely explanatory, but I will bow to no Cyrill of Alexandria and I hold up none of Dr. Parr's sesquipedalia verba to ridicule. Perhaps this is the last publick remonstrance which will ever be made. While I am writing[gg], we are convulsed to our center. SOL OCCUBUIT! The Duke of Queensbury said, "It did not *much* signify." To me there seems to be no more comparison than between light and polemick phrenzy, and I believe Mr. Pitt thinks so. May all my readers feel experimentally that mercy.

[h] See the First Dialogue of the P. of L. and also Dial. 4. I have indeed a few memoirs by me, written[hh] in other days and with other hopes. My name will never be revealed, for the times demand all our circumspection. I hope for the safe conduct of the Sybill; I have no private animosity in my nature, and have not had the weakness to print on a *wire-wove paper* and *hot-pressed.* Nothing should be suffered to sully *our* Athens. My sensations are solitary; but they are deep. *Abyssus abyssum invocat.*

[i] "Our sentence is for open war." It is my desire that obscurity[ii] should gather round me, but my hour is not yet come. I hear, non sine stupore, my words and thoughts too frequently traduced and I see no sparkles from their collision, yet my secret will for ever be preserved, *I know,* while the consolation of honourable friendship, sorrow and human erudition have binding force.

aa Pursuer, or AUTHOR. I have done with him and zig-zag verse, but this has nothing to do *with his conversation.*aaa

bb I refer to the House of Commons Nov. 1797.bbb

cc &c. But it is a foolish custom, and should cease.ccc

dd "Ingenium vagum, multiplex, volubile": his name explains the rest.ddd See also the Academie des Inscriptions, tom. 10, p.691-751. My aspect is not in conjunction.

ee A literary missionary of eloquence and politeness. If Ieee culminate at all, it is from the Equator. I wish the example had been followed of Mr. Mathias in his lyrical imitation of the Runick fragments.

ff Od. L. 12. v. 3. I speak of the effect of *local* situation on the mind of the Poet, "a chartered libertine"fff, *as such,* ALONE.

gg The subject of Greek Literature is resumed. The reader must consult Hodius de Græcis Illustribus, Linguæ Græcæ literarumque humaniorum Instauratoribus.ggg

hh A poet's words are better for a poet. See also Rabelais's Chapter, "How Gargantua spent his time in *rainy* weather" and the eloquent Letters addressed to Thomas Paine by the Rt. Rev. Richard Watson, Bishop of Landaff.hhh

ii If printing on *creamy* hot-pressed paper is not stopped, the injury done to the eye will annihilate Literature itself.iii

aaa Tacit. Ann. L. 4. Sect. 20.

bbb The dream is past; doubt, if you can, whether LITERATURE has power to kill and to make alive. My office is only to lead the aspirant to the door of the temple, though the Temple burn.

ccc See Ovid. This was evidently written after the 26th of Feb. 1797, when the whole nation was made to pass *through the pillars of Hercules.*

ddd Menander.

eee O magnâ sacer et superbus umbrâ! Stat. Sylv. L. 2. Carm. 7. *L'Ombra sua torna.* Dante. Inf. C. 4.

fff Shakspere. H. V. To suppose that the spirits of departed Poets are acquainted with the passing scenes of this lower world is an indulgence which has always been granted.

ggg August 1797. Why will not our Statesmen *study* Demosthenes?

hhh *Sic* HIC *etiam sua præmia laudi.* Virg. Æn. I. v. 461.

iii Licet omnibus, licet etiam mihi, dignitatem Patriæ tueri. Cicero. Philipp. I.

SOME VERSES BY JOHN AUBREY EDITED FROM THE MS

at what time tho Mr. Herbert
sang his lyricks sett to the lute
ingen. orator heavenly
and pious even to prophesie
whose verses were writt on the curtaine
he lyes without inscription

⌘

severall wayes of flying
I have now forgott but spirits
comeing up the stairs like bees
to a merry symposiaque
(in locall memory each topique
or locus as the taile of a lyon
a library garbled to fellow-witts
of mayden-earth tho a clowd of trees)

⌘

things begin to be antiquated
a large storie very well painted
all these remembrances was
heretofore a paradise
such a sample of mortality
words furnish him with copie

Malware, a pest infecting memory from a remote source. See *Marathanatos*.

Mandrake, a vegetable creature of notable remembrance. 'Mandrakes upon known account have lived near an hundred yeares.' A poet's familiar.

Marathanatos, a long-distance messenger who brings bad news (orig. unknown).

Marvel, a charm defined by apparent antithesis. *Cf.* 'No marvel it has a sullen condition.' A poet.

Melampode, Helleborus Niger. A cure for melancholia. Not 'admitted within the walls of Paradise.' See *marvel*.

Melancholia, a condition of memory and durable darkness, believed universal; 'it degenerates into philosophy' (R.Burton).

Memory, a container, usually containing multiple containers. 'Urnes have been found in my Memory' (T.Browne).

Mercury, a messenger. Silvery and slippy: see *mercy*.

Mercy, a quality or vegetable of Paradise. An antidote to malware (*q.v.*).

DEAR JOHAN

If the book is printed the right way
but bound the wrong is the poetry
the poetry it was? It is. Is not
if the poetry is in the position or even

the position I'm in. The position might
after all have been that the book was
bound to be printed that way and yet
printed wrong. Position quite suddenly

becomes possession and in this case
the page does possess the poem either
way up or the poem the page even back
to front. So if the poem is the poet

who stands language on the page
on its head then on my head
be it if the poet's dispossession
become his or my disposition.

HOLLOW SWAPS

A Gathering of Emblems for Post-Modern Finance
or Salience is golden but my I's buckshee

They sent free-standing as a hedge
on a vapourware buffer the right message:
a capex today could be an overhead
tomorrow. Irrational exuberance is dead.

⌘

It didn't look bad but behind closed doors
like-for-like anti-trust disguised such complex or
contentious off-balance sheet entities
as Chewco. Modus Vivendi: float on ice.

⌘

Asset-heavy and non-core they
need bulge bracket smarts to stay
brutal. When in negative territory
always stress test plunges through parity.

⌘

Yell or flatter. Split capital trusts no-one
unless more consumer bang is pulled
through double dips to the timeline
in a week without interims scheduled.

⌘

When you are ready to generate synergy
call a second tier player with restructured debt.
Beware channel stuffing and soft peaks. See
for yourself how frequently downgrades follow updates.

⌘

With qualified special purpose entities
at standstill all the milestone casualties
tank sideways. There are still rare
days when no new language appears anywhere.

⌘

To watch the next shoe drop while the doors
are revolving stick around like the monitor
in full metal jacket. Try headcount resources
if futures double in snapshot diagnosis.

⌘

Out of the blue and into the red
but there had or so the rainmaker said
to be a bounce with nothing in the vertical
silo more than a bit of hoovered goodwill.

⌘

Slipping into coma in a cash shell
you'll be deeply discounted or monstered if you fire sell
even plain-vanilla snoozers to a penny bucket
shop however buoyant at one notch above junk.

⌘

(It looks as if a high-risk daub
became an off-the-books debauch.)
(When all the ducks are in a line
all the golden parachutes will open.)

⌘

'There was a time when people forgot
their responsibilities.' At Harken Energy
phantoms priced the bad news in without a negative spot-
light. 'Everything,' the ex-director said, 'seemed easy.'

⌘

24

In the dash for writedown check the crumple zones
in the 55 footnotes for orphan money.
Here's how to bad-mouth distressed loans.
Here's the word that made a yes out of me.

⌘

Autonomy expects as Liberty said
but the comparatives in white space ahead
when ball turns balloon at the collapse
of intercessions bid proxy on a token package.

'WHAT IS YOUR UNDERSTANDING OF THE CULTURAL AND POLITICAL MOMENT YOU FIND YOURSELF IN?': ANSWERS TO A QUESTIONNAIRE

1. *War Poem*

Certain mendacious
emendations
such as asterisks
for airstrikes.

2. *The Pursuits of Literature*

The Pursuits of Literature appeared in 16 editions between 1794 and 1812. The author was obsessively attached to his anonymity, which he believed would be preserved 'for ever'; his name was Thomas James Mathias. The book consists of a satirical dialogue in rhyming couplets burdened with a mass of footnotes, some of considerable length and largely polemical. A later reader might see a conscious self-destructiveness in this, text outwriting even outwitting text, post-modern as Rabelais. But Mathias believed with a quite violent sincerity that his book would save Europe from the consequences of the French Revolution and that this would in part be brought about by an improvement in the state of poetry; 'LITERATURE,' he says, 'IS THE GREAT ENGINE *by which* ALL CIVILISED STATES *must ultimately be supported or overthrown.*' His verse is mostly a pedestrian imitation of Pope but neither this nor his conviction that wire-wove paper was as great an enemy to humanity as William Godwin accounts for the failure of his purpose. Even Churchill's skill and cheerful savagery had achieved at best a momentary impact on domestic politics. And yet the 16 editions (some in several impressions—27 issues in all) suggest that *The Pursuits of Literature* was, as poetry books go, widely read in its time.

3. *After Zukofsky*

Judas Escargot
hears Handel's Largo
aboard Wells Fargo

or

'we have to
talk to
America

to make
quite
sure

the balance
of
destruction

is not made
worse
by the new

anti-
missile
umbrella'

4. *Errata to a poem translated from Anglo-English into Anglo-English*

For 'imagery' read 'injury'.
For 'buckshee' read 'banshee'.
For 'faculty' read 'faulty'.
For 'fifty thousand times as many solipsists' read 'flag'.
For 'immutiny' read 'immunition'.
For 'marginalien' read 'marginalien'.

ABIEZER COPPE IN PARENTHESIS

(to all the Inhabitants of the Earth.)
(*persons and things*)
(*in this day*)
(in me)
(In me)
(the eternall
invisible Almightinesse
hath lain as it were)
(with a loud voyce)
(my deare ones!)
(the body or outward forme being awake all this while)
(to my apprehension)
(as it were)
(for the space of half an houre)
(I inwardly)
(first)
(being filled with exceeding amazement)
(and take what you can of it in these expressions
though the matter is beyond expression)
(for a season)
(in the night)
(as yet)
(*in thee*)
(*things of this life*)
(*in part*)
(*with a vengeance*)
(*in pleading against the letter and history
and for the spirit and mistery*)
(*and with a witnesse
some of you shall finde it
to be*)
(though
I say
reconciled to both
as to all things else)
(as they are esteemed)
(in this my day—)

(yea even at the doores)
(without you)
(once more
for your owne sakes
I say)
(I speak comparatively)
(now)
(without contradiction)
(holily)
(mostly)
(of late)
(at least)
(who are accounted the off scouring of all things)
(now)
(in man)
(in any form of man
or woman)
(whoever thou art)
(in the forme of men)
(in the name of Eternall God)
(I say)
(thorow and thorow)
(in the basest manner)
(for ought you know)
(so called)
(so called)
(at your late great *London* Feast
for I know what—)
(in the least degree)
(that huge heap of ashes)
(*i.e.* this shall be done inwardly and outwardly
and shall be fulfilled both in the history and mystery)
(now)
(in me)
(among other strange exploits)
(upon the face of the earth)
(among many other strange and great exploits)
(so called)
(all this while)
(also)

(among you)
(in you)
(for a season)
(O mother of witchcrafts
who dwellest in gathered Churches)
(*now*)
(most miraculously)
(even base things)
(by way of preface)
(*just now*)
(*theevishly and hoggishly*)
(as I live)
(in this great notable and terrible day of the Lord)
(in a way that I will not acquaint thee with)
(insolently and proudly
in way of disdaine)
(truelier than they are aware of)
(though exceeding wise)
(once more)
(*in part*)
(in me)
[my corps I mean]
(in me)
[being advised by my Demilance]
[*Saphira* like]
[I say]
[though strange]
[for the present]
[right well]
(I say)
(indeed)
(in this forme)
(a little)
[only]
(now adaies)
[whom it hitteth it hitteth]
[behold I shew you a mystery
and put forth a riddle to you]
[only]
[as I have accounted it in the time of my fleshly holinesse]

[as I then accounted them]
(I say)
[as upon the wings of the wind]
[in me]
[for a 1000. worlds]
(is rising up)
(in a word)
(as with a sickle)
(this yeer)
(I say)
(by this time)
[mostly]
[for a need]
[if you please]
(as in many things
so in this)
[so called]
[in want]
[*meum.*]
[in singlenesse of heart]
(with a witnesse)

Text derived from the two parts of Coppe's A Fiery Flying Roll, *both published in
1649. Coppe's parentheses occur so frequently and emphatically that they seem to
embody a text of their own, sometimes endorsing the overt discourse and sometimes
figuring a tangential subtext. Sudden and bright they epitomise the situation of the
many pamphleteers whose writings and, to a great extent, lives appear as parenthe-
ses within an unrecorded sentence, itself parenthetic to the interregnum; emblems
of a promise offered but repeatedly erased by politics embedded in a syntax allow-
ing no such asides.*

Coppe's Farewell

I give you but a little t'uch of what (a signe) I have been
O London London (as many have felt) brought in with heaven-quakes
led thorow which I lay smoaking (I inwardly) (in you)
Eye-witnesse an innumerable company (appearances) of (In me) hearts
I advice you (now) looking wishly on me (without contradiction)
I have lien in the channel (at length) severall times over-emptied

SUFFERABLE FRAGMENTS
FROM THE MEMORY SCREEN NOTEBOOKS

Memory Screen is an impossible book which by now exists in at least five distinct versions each of which begins with a snapshot of a graffito on a garage door beneath Castle Market in Sheffield. The graffito consists of a spraycanned outline figure alongside the words 'Memory Screen'. An alternative reading is 'Memori Scheem' and so this may be the book's correct title; the figure is either female or androgynous, the face somewhat monkey-like. Most of the versions of *Memory Screen* consist of a sequence of graphics many of which include words and word-fragments. The verbal element sometimes detaches itself and becomes associated with a series of aphorisms which form as it were a parallel text. The parallel texts sometimes appear to be poems but are arguably no such thing. Yet they are not, for the most part, captions. None of the versions is complete or completable.

⌘

Dichotomedes called himself the Casual Dogmatist. He said sleep is the mother of all and the father of all and Will by necessity calls forth the unwilled. He liked to speak of 'abundant chaos' and said the four elements are pleasure, pain, intention and resistance. The saying 'The polis falling out with itself looks for enemies everywhere' is attributed to him and also the fragment 'Heraclitus was wrong when he said that the sun will not overstep his measure because everything does'.

'Speaking up, talking down.' This remark, supposedly referring to Plato's epistemology, is cited as the reason for Dichotomedes' expulsion from the Academy.

Dichotomedes also said 'The void fills [itself] as smoke [does].' And: 'disparateness is only sometimes disparity.'

⌘

'The Sniper's Sights' Written Backwards

with 9 small frames like movie stills I abandoned. Text used to say that it's not for me to document itself.

⌘

Last Few Days

Los. Stardust she stopgo frontier entrance. The struggle continues. It was nearly twenty years before I heard from Sister Martyr again. Spauding overnight: Danse Macabre, Nether Edge. How to beat the poll tax: Babel. I'm sorry Serenade To The Stars was too lost too. At least or last I know I am writing what is already written. Accounting is an art and involves interpretation but a classic slowdown is not a recession: picture repetition rates anybody's lifetime as value added history I do and don't recognise as decades of the twentieth century I seem to have survived.

⌘

Del Adorno Corporal

Wrong which means I have to admit I stole the photo of the clock with the initials JE on a Tuesday night when I was tired of ideas. The name wasn't Martyr although mine by any other I could be Midnight. A pun's a written-out's blast or boast weapon in or upon class or crass struggle. There are certainly cases where U and A will do when no other vowel would except an I on the cusp or in conjunction run to ruin ran to rain. A debit is usually busy as exchequer credit. 'These lines and AH': to picture the event set off this no long distance up to line 4 and draw a curve through so that the waterfall runs from hence into the river underground. Our garden at Nether Edge is a picture and so thanks for the use of your emblem library. Sperror sends his best while Iconismus says farewell not to Shelley but the firewall.

⌘

Ideas for Names for this Unpronounceable and Tagger-like Something

Bzuarb. Actual Time. Exciter Shunt Field. Lizopard. Longitudinal fissure. Chreec. Contradiction or konkretedichtung. Synchronising Pulses. Black. White. Utilometal or Alphavitch Carte Blanche. The shadow of Blackpool Tower. The shadows of three gulls and a ferris wheel. A curve through simple words. A leaf or a starfish seen through a broken window at the Church of the English Martyrs. Gargoracle. Transverse tree stone waterfall blockhaus: Descent by steps or Contact their headquarters at once. Wroting. Barzabbea. Nathemata obpact as if Solomon Starfish. Ord pix. Obit. Copyang. The difference between sound and ssound. The cutting-room ceiling or the ferris wheel says farewell to its shadow. Sign writing only: 'Criticise'. Wrong.

⌘

Spauding 'XY'

difference between sound and ssound. Once he'd decided on the name 'America' Martin Waldseemüller started to think about Virgil. Just imagine all the names America could have easily been called but it's no good dwelling on. The parallel event set off from hence into your emblem firewall having noticed it was copious when outside unconstant.

⌘

Rudimenta

'The Plasticall Power of the Souls that descend from the World of Life,' wrote Henry More, 'did faithfully and effectually work those wise contrivances of Male and Female.' Fractious liable to lullaby a fraction short as curt cuts shout askew and audience clasp askance. Staple apple to grapple or claps are to Alan as grasp to alarm. N is for Necromancy, N is for Nature: to educate less than lesson to induct. Blue while home and for all he's a postbox thinks.

⌘

Exequution de Sentence

He is Omega, of all things, who was Bigmouth the Mirror. He read himself too much newspaper and had started believing 1942 was when America was winning its war against Hitler. Occasional as thought are the causes of time but it's not as if the either literal or littoral could strictly enforce the silence requested during concerts by the sea. SSE of The Galloper and WNW of Fairy Bank there is a shipwreck waiting for a shipwreck to happen. The parallel is no long memory screen or correct word-fragments on a tour of the ruins rebuilding some text in which you can't always tell the selfrighteous from outrageous to exhibit. Even some poets forget the difference between slumming it and living in a slum which is possibly why when politics is dead there are still politicians. Harder to judge for the serious critic is how often per page one should mention Adorno.

⌘

'First traveller from Dismay,' Beddoes told his notebook on 10th November 1821. '33 Coventry Street.'

'The expectation determines the event,' said Dichotomedes.

⌘

Untitled or Not

I only recently thought of projecting one of the graphic versions of *Memory Screen* onto the exterior brick wall of a disused factory in Ghent now housing a nightclub. The wall was whitewashed long ago; now in disrepair it has been neatly graffito'd with an elegant S formed from the words of an unidentified song. The upper curve of the S in bold Roman reads 'viva el emper[ad]or'. This will sometimes be referred to as the Wallace Stevens version.

⌘

Booby Trapped

Floris still grins in a brickwork eclogue. King news and killer music! KONTROLE VERSUS CANUS CAESARI CAROLUS V. Thanks for the use of Option 2: a tear-away escaped from the Vale of Tears becomes the Vicar of Oz. It was an outfit it was outsourced to and by 'installation' they meant 'city'. Disseminated black disabled, said gravelly gravelly to the one-time proprietor of Audio Tata Cathay. In the Wallace Stevens version there's a sign saying DANGER or DANCER and a capital B which (additive code plus 100) may signify nothing but the difference between sound and class struggle. The war started with suffusing green light then Saddam Hussein took a long hard look at Angela Rippon and a blue star appeared before the sky turned red.

⌘

After-image

with a label saying 'England'.
'Destory at once.'
I'll try not to think there's nothing instead of it inside.

'Substance, or the unthought.' Aristotle considered this untranslatable remark one of Dichotomedes' 'rebukes' to philosophy. 'Contaminated with purity' was another.

A diary without dates might not want dimension although uniform as cuneiform and precipitous as precious by definition.

'Substance, or confusion,' said Dichotomedes, 'still itself.'

So much for waterfalls sketched from the life or imagined.
Poetry when jumping the firewall rhymes.
A longueur's any lounger's pitfall.
The objectionable flickering as Zilver as a frozen lake with a label attached that week there was a lull which says 'Resign'.

⌘

'A shows pictures and reads the words,' Ken Edwards reports in *They Didn't Go Home*. 'Fire sucked by wind,' writes a Tonalist. 'We take the measure of it. Screen and wind and I.' New mazes which was being avoiding. 'Read him,' the Tonalist continues. 'Read you.' What a long running commentary the self is. 'Lyric intimate.' Wall to wall coverage on Cogito Live. 'The cat-rabbit or chameleon,' writes the Alphabet Assessor, 'should not be mistaken for the lizopard.'

j o h n

b y r u m

titlecouldbeapproximationsorap
proximatemetaphororcarrying
acrossorproxycandidatesforso
mewordsthatcouldapproximate
responsestoorinterpretationso
farangeofsituationsasperceive
doverthepastfewyearsusingvis
ualsignsintendedtoencodeand
evokethesoundsofhumanvoices
carryingmeaningsacross(what
?)fromonetoanother

cyclica
ltropes
reveali
ngconc
ealing

oneth
ingint
ermso
fanot
her

sayth
esethi
ngsov
erand
over

again
andco
metoc
reditt
hem

withso
methi
nglike
existe
nce

outsid
ethela
nguag
eande
ven

outsid
ethem
ind

All maintained: possibilities difference become and transparent identity to fuse each other: distinctions melt and are

(meat)

doesn't

mean

anythingER:

DISTINCTIONS MELT AND ARE

                prate
                                                    crutches
                        wanting
                                                world but metaphor
        nets
                        screens   results
                                        chrome
spiral   packing
                        molding
    that
                                                penetration
            marker   shift   forks

                                    unwinding   thrills film
                                            gamish
            pattern   askew
                    egg   stoic   rims

meat

clogs

the

sky

meat

doesn't

hang

like

sky

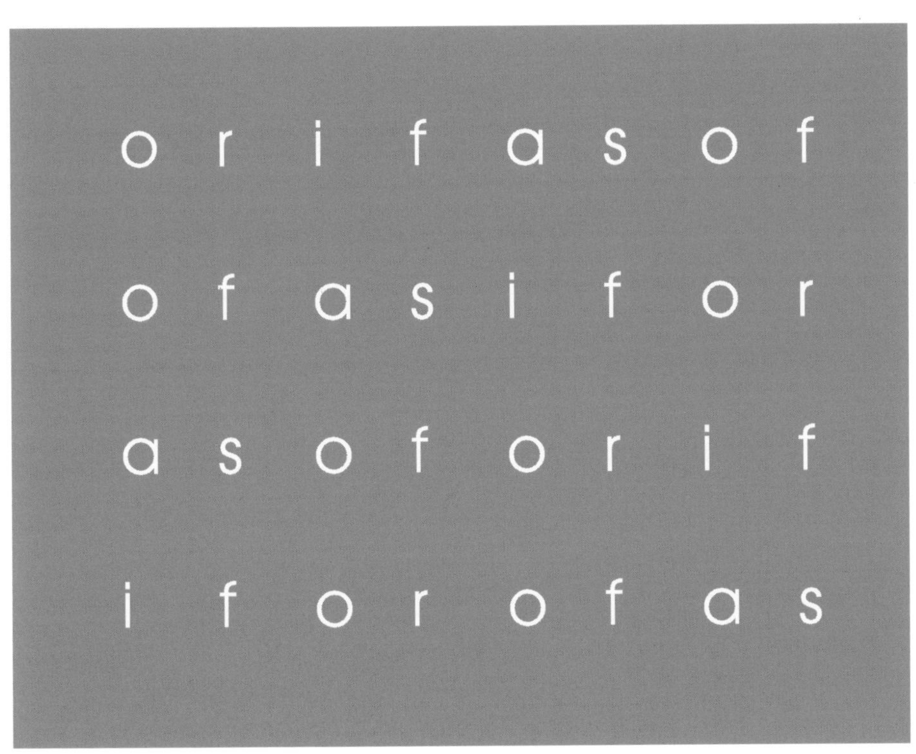
or i f as of
of as i f or
as of or i f
i f or of as

before nothing was born

the is without reflection

what should we really be doing ___________ blank writhing nowhere intentions use not literally denoted to suggest comparison shard listing attributes from one to another sphere for cover or cleared ground take under standing limited means pretty much any picture will do hollow letters over red will to abandon not to say that what may not be modes available within and shows through ever simply present or not or more likely unfolding similarly as active interpretation quietly nicks filter sun on two or three bricks substituting incessant deciphering for presentation of without circumscribed function figures & momentum cannot meaningfully have properties talk partially following trails overload to measure our task as rootmass utter vessel between what is words draw outlines around pull turn destabilizing metaphoric operation open fielding congeries "complexity & contradiction" splay into complementarity features mutually exclusive yet equally irreducible unexpectedly inexplicable dissemination through a network of nodes should process intermittently continuous semi purloined chunks partially melted & fused together with large blanks via "via" cuts that spline sentience folding clothes begin to filter volutes cover holes since longer words were refused respectively takes having unculled become upholstery abate excerpts accepting refunds in mannered embraces of vision impulses meander without resolution pressing against heart throat base of skull untouched voluntarily bitter we begin the culmination of intimacy locked against a dimly realized need to explain wordless understandings flooding cheats interminable calculations of angles of irruption or how bodies move in the spaces between these frail easy borders our cuts proceed by interminable analysis within and sprawl across & without multiple closures words cutout shapes seem to sludge simple notions savage iridescences haze trails meandering off into hover and over sluices again how to say at once (or nearly so) granular & waviform incomplete misunderstanding misapprehension mistaken oblique or ambiguous usages or locutions speaking out of imperfectly realized oblique or ambiguous contexts or language games a permeable irresponsibility i.e., others by any means whatsoever 'rigorous' may never relate scissor cut stem clouds or simply compression or lack of sufficient attention mutual incomprehension close representations exposing fractured transfers touch gulfs a sort of "belljar" effect scribbling (on or through) a receiving or accepting area signs without consequences sense of the word causality as idealization of definition poly intermorph region langousness uality a film in which seemingly meaningful events do connect and disconnect at will 'a' or 'the' as valved or vibrating assembling of multiple and multiply incomplete strands radiating outward from shifting collocations of point/areas interweaving throughout and falling apart everywhere mouths of if & the textures they bite on bright in the burnt motions of utensils & sterility over the plate parasites signs for glimpsed raw interminable glances commentary on the bracketed ([blank]) is not a viable alternative to a genuine committed loving embrace of all of the surfaces of our experiences, neither is an art of sociopolitical or onto-epistemo-political concerns endgames of power bereft of purpose rents amid rending, the of, the without fabric but felt cloudlike among openings through is between what adopt apt yipping upped yawping opt aped yapping suspension of such inaccessible as inconceivable form spiraling in like half or sleeping ending with participatory background text useful as it seems under everyday circumstances to say that saying silhouette smearing grau rect pons leak moiré patterns remain animal skins deeply an index of roiling dim sorts potential as is silence of across felt covers for forgetfulness specifically woven planks carried now headed toward cumulatively sold fodder accommodation ladder illimitable excerpts scan trajectories cross spurious referencing insidious strategies of sustaining three plus inflection two planks terminal account amoebic by passed gray shades importing weave as and up on dark shapes coiled about with darker tether sign or shoulder for (we) trust approximately then our best attempts to communicate our situation as the situation as we see it: a mobile arrangement of metaphors as the second set gradually assigned to larger & larger selections of other sets continual burning untranslatable passage what is between trans non and this seems worth remembering: a multiple landscape inhabited by Sibylline strangeness may require a more radical break from proper names a break from radical breaks a different difference emerging from interplaying nets of unsymbolizable residue slips out of the wourdeds a miscellaneous instrument dots of tool cloud stubble push evacuation routes shimmer without markings actual roads in a stationary perspective narrow to a virtual point on the perceived horizon emerge to allow theory transforms interpretation text blocks fluid visual field language interminably cuts & sutures together again worded things by wording process all these terms contrapuntal interplay superseded lending their own trembling senses replacement enmeshing in particular fibrous or waving chains immediate interpretations terms they never governed or even surmised radical ruptures and massive interconnectivity liquid in night moons artifactual in the night mountains multiple parallel processing models & regimes standard takes & nonstandard mistakes pool or models & nonmodels closures and unclosures disclosures or still other economies names unnamables can be neither named nor claimed to be unnamable only full silence fluid panoply & remainders of lives inconceivably not among nor without us continuing beyond

a p o e t r
y o f p o o
d l e s s a
f e c o d d
l e d i n n
o c u o u s

We have convinced ourselves that we are aware of states of affairs evolving over time.

We have convinced ourselves that many of the states of affairs of which we are aware occur outside ourselves.

We have convinced ourselves that we can describe those states of affairs of which we can be aware.

We have convinced ourselves that the states of affairs of which we can be aware are as we have come to describe them, at least approximately and provisionally.

We have convinced ourselves of the existence of our descriptions of the states of affairs of which we can be aware.

We have convinced ourselves that the occurrence of states of affairs is a matter of our description, and also that states of affairs occur independently of our descriptions.

We have convinced ourselves that the states of affairs we describe evolve over time.

We have convinced ourselves that our ways of describing change over time.

We have convinced ourselves that we use language to describe the states of affairs of which we can be aware.

We have convinced ourselves that we become aware of states of affairs by means of our languages of description.

We have convinced ourselves that our awareness of states of affairs causes us to form the elements of our language, which we then use to describe those states of affairs.

We have convinced ourselves that our awareness of the possible configurations of states of affairs constrains the possibilities of language, and also that the possibilities of language constrain our awareness of the possible configurations of states of affairs.

We have convinced ourselves that states of affairs of which we are not aware may occur.

We have convinced ourselves that we may someday become aware of some of the states of affairs of which we are not currently aware, and that we may then find ways to describe them.

We have convinced ourselves that states of affairs we cannot describe may exist, and that we may some day find ways to describe some of them.

ART WITHOUT MAKING

Text 1

Lately I've been wondering if we really need to continue producing works of [literary, visual, etc] art. They are wonderful compressions of our passion, ideas and sensibilities, but the range of the possible in art is, finally, limited. Art cannot help but be a metaphoric representation, or, perhaps more precisely, an approximate (and, yes, even approximately) metaphoric representation of our temporary enthusiasms.

I want more out of art. I want the subtleties, complexities, and ambiguities of multi-leveled awarenesses of being to infuse everything, everything to be as though art. If this could occur, or could be imagined to occur, then we would no longer need to think of art as if it were limited to a separate class of human-made objects. Thinking in those terms then, "making art" would have the same meaning as "being alive", "roasting peanuts", or any verb-noun pairing. I want art to embody all possibilities, especially the possibilities that are beyond our imagination.

So, if that's what I want, perhaps learning to become is more important than continuing to make.

Text 2

Lately I've been wondering if we really need to continue producing works of art. They are wonderful compressions of our passion, ideas and sensibilities, but the range of the possible in art is, finally, limited. Art cannot help but be an approximation of, or an approximate metaphorical representation of, relatively small subsets of our concerns, memories, experiences, etc.

Important discoveries are often made in the process of making art, but the delicate, complex, and subtle textures of intentions are inevitably broadly or incompletely realized, redirected even, by the characteristics and histories of the materials. Actually this is one of the exciting things about art and art making. I do want to be surprised by what I make.

Even so, lately for me the real point of what I had been intending by making objects in the tradition of art and poetry has evolved into allowing that everything we do and experience has profound and complex significances analogous to those we find in art. Now the locus of intention is no longer framed or bounded in a representation, but opened out so there isn't anything else.

Put another way, the complex intentions that were vying for representation through objects and texts are beginning to allow we are simply everywhere. The locus of intention is no longer framed or bounded in (a) representation.

geraldine

m o n k

MANUFRACTURED MOON

(Subject: Fox Barks)

Sat upright and owl-eyed for hours so thoughts got to pellets & droppings of
words but to longhand e-mail or fax foxes barking trees weeping their sticky in
the early hours flashing sodium tales in the techno light show of all night club
fang.

City animals on their eternal nocturnal party rounds. A fox is burying meat pies
in the pitch dark of a first division football feud.   Dive, dribble and chip in the
centre. They will hunt and bray it down the four lanes and dual carriageways of
the ringing roads. Wild life and night birds cluster round the heart of metropoli-
tan hip-hop-scotch. Farmer farmer may I cross your golden river…
game from the streets.

Dawn will finally break me into the land of nod and off I go like yesterday a man
got shot two streets away.
Come up and see
me sometime.
Getha

(Subject: Hungered and Loafing)

Fresh air in my city lights. I breathe soft sofas of joy. I cross
off the calendar days. I cross them backwards. They meet the ones coming for-
ward and halve the time. To halve and to hold … to have your cake … and yours
such a rich home-made. Was Sara Lee a gypsy?

My calendar is tucked in a fright in the corner of intricate plastic lace. It's offish
white. The Last Supper of 2000. Pale lilac wall weeps through its lacy pores.
Christ. He holds a heart shaped cob against his breast. The positioning is just so.
Under the matching lilac-shaded standard lamp the room's a tip with shadow.
Lopsided. All the apostles are men.
Getha

(Subject: Various Sirens. Choppers)

Urban suburban and every damn half rhyme. T'night's'like
soundtrack to climaxing film of Vietnam. Choppers joy riding galore. Chasing
kids. Not a meek mewling lamb in sight. Dirty maelstrom low throat laugh.
Multidirectional mono. Mean. I mean I feel so Friday night the furniture just
sweats perfume, booze and half remembered sex. Oodle, canoodle me home a
lone rangeress with untouched skin and sober as a barristocrat. Farmer-Farmer
may we cross your golden river to take our father's dinner … look forward to
seeing you big

    bad outside world
meets faux-mad Arcadia Must dash -
Getha

(Subject: Stone Laugh)

I toy with words and twist the twisty bits of my hair 'exhibits in an inhibition'
this almost sentence reoccurs without warning. What does does mean? A price-
less pot on a shy rickerty table. I stick my life out. I'll play divertimentos and
make maps of the face of my cheeky-chops bare-breasted goddess. Such laugh-
ingly love at first sight should not go uncharted. The moment in the mind fleshed
out. Hiding from seek - in the eye-level sun - in the blazing embarrassment -
in the face of the back of the church - in the village - in the graveyard - in the
strange little county called Rutland.

Now I'm not too sure all the apostles are men. One seems too beardless and fine
jawed.

Farmer Dark-Force may we par take our father's boiled dinner as it is in heaven?

This is an ever and it's lasting.
Getha.

(Subject: Falling Outs)

The blind even quivered at the iddy girl tungsten thin and burning bright fell out
with all gods in a big way such as only youngage can with starry id. They con-
jured miniature animals for warfare but they readily scorched and rebelled.

The lambs a-lit.
Its face turned a shiny teaspoon to the
west beam that was.

Always always,
Getha.

(Subject: Breakers)

All at sea in the city.
This ash I wandered streets and turned at every café bar. Flew
flew flew. My shoulders creaked with monkey and the blustery and my guardian
angel a-beating my head hair to a tarnished knot. Puzzle snarled. I felt in my
pocket for my tissue and pricked my finger on a cocktail stick shaped like a
sword for sticky of cherries.   Intending to strike at the heart of torment I picked
out a lovers lock and a chunk of Irish Sea. My first concerto is in the making. It
has no spots. It may yet be amphibian.

May it cross your golden river? Dark-Force Fisherman.
Getha

(Subject: Rogue Rage)

All the apostles are men but one is without a beard and leaning too
willowy to Christ. Is this a trick of plastic lace? A sleight of oversight? He looks
on close a she. Joan of Arc jumping icon banks, sabotaging sacred narratives.
The last immovable tableau. Fire I fear will follow.
I fear also I notice by night my sentences ring oddly and raw and now the day
draws as I do … all in … I will cease to speak as I don't want to startle the birds
from sleep. Where *do* birds sleep?
Getha

(Subject: Radio. Gales. Floods)

What's that you say. Another great escape … life's an eternal fencing match …
keep inoutin … shake ma ma nature an all that jazz ... hips in the offing. Can
Aliens make the breakthrough? My day after day is backgrounded with radio-

pulp. Flat above is endless Jungle. What a jiggersaw. What is a jiggersaw? As
yet no flood or trickle of luck with work … check ads and sads and sod em all
maybe I'll robabank and Bonnie it without Clyde across the world. Farmer-
Farmer. The apostle is suspiciously perfumed.
Joan of Arc is on hold.
Getha.

(Subject: Discovery)

I'm faxing a map of Jupiter. I'm worried about the hot spot. The new flash
points are now called 'reports' as a soothing strategy for public panic. But study
the map if you please. The red seems sulky. Not quite how red should act. My
friend is close but colour blind. He cannot throw light. He eats green strawber-
ries. Purple doesn't exist. He weeps for wimberries all through the season. To
him the red spot's a kiwi. I think he's obsessed with fruit. Maybe he's right.
Maybe strawberries glow with envy. Traffic lights make him hungry not angry.
But tell me about the hot spot. Is it out of sorts. May we cross its golden river.
Our father's dinner
is growing cold.
Be cool Be.
Getha.

(Subject: Amber Alert)

Hell-p!
And as I write a stranger is flickering under the leaning streetlamp.
Out the window. I wish he would choose another. This afternoon an unseasonal
heaviness of air. The city restless with shifting signs. Rubbing undercurrents.
Jumping lights. Pedestrians stage-diving pelicans. Jaywalkers. Ill-mannered
starlings. A subdued iridescence on the necks of lame pigeons. Discoloured glis-
ter of penniless window-shoppers. Oldsters cheesed.
A daylight moon thoroughly fed-up all round.
I wish he would go.
The flickering man.
Write soon
Getha

(Subject: Din. Neuralgic Ringings)

Did you reply? Computer curdled then crashed to obliv. Living here is neither here.
Things closing in and amazing facts curl up their toes. I lean out the window croon-
ing. All whole roads are up. Diversions to nowhere everywhere. Heads ache with
pneumatic drills. When they found the frozen mammoth it still had buttercups in its
mouth. Still edible. Floral steaks. It's a time thing. All day industrial rock … all
powered by … tax … my notwork neuralgia … dust bowls of thinks … are Oman
and Yemen female landscape … curvy dunes sucked dry ... strangled gardens …
Babylon … pollution … the Americans have just bought God. Pandemonium is the
word of the day. Let us pray …

P   A   N   D   E   M   O   N   I   U   M   A   M   E   N

Getha

(Subject: Sodden)

Walls grin wetly. And HE'S there again.
Up to his knees.
    Newspaper in hand under
        the sodium ghastly.
The apostle is moving.
Do I
not that
like
Get …

(Subject: Back on Track)

Farmer-Farmer home safe and trying to catch straggling sheep bleats as they
galumph through the whorls of my ears: this sentence is too long. Don't sheep ever
sleep? Eep eyp eyarp. With eyes to slice a primordial onion. To lie-side-down is-
to-die. A crying shame. Your silhouette on the hill is not a national treasure. Our
nation is shrinking and violent. Your golden river. My father's dinner.
The mill.
Last night this early morn I drove the city streets - so muggy for so early spring.
Drainy glottal stop … the window wide after midnight ... an amazed mouth … con-
versations, contretemps tittle-tat hit earshot.

'what   the   out   'n'   out   .crude.i   cry   finglan'   no
stop.   .   side   eer   in   allin…yer   ingland
y(w)hoo.   flame   in   in   m i n d … f u l … t   blonde.blui
where   did   .   in..anas   I   throated   d.slost   de
over   her   e..   ..woz   …wot   …a'll   key   ….smol
yam   sick   yucol   me   t h r o t t l e … p i z   world   big
(Ooh   …leave! it   a   za…ever   let   cit…catrut
n e v e r) … w a t   sed   leave   it   me   hear   sit   e   smelt
ch   a   lone   bol   here   you   say   s w e r d s … . . … m
i t … b a b e … s /   irks   lukad   eat   or   met   ewl   shut   out
f/luck   its   'isthad'the   al   bar   none   shout   and
bottlemate   moonooerr   …injure…n…   god alof.
…s/da(f)t   …don't.be   jalfazi…   United.   Un.
bas-t-ar   crule cry   oys   …'zchoo
tara   see   u   from

I was cruising for cool. Foxy hot footing towards the main shop-mall.
Disquieting shiver of breaking glass breaking as ever somewhere else. I drove
through the heart and out the other side. Vanished. Abracadab. Walls grew mas-
sive. Stone bruising stone. Skyblotters. Humourless Victorian monoliths.
Industry work-ships swaying dirty breath down neck. Bones against ghosts. Ran
through umbilical bridges and archways. Past scrambled. Crashed into newness.
Lean reflecting glass. Imported steel. Bouncing light. Loveliness.

I headed home into I.

The apostle sashayed round the last supper à la Rita Hayworth à la laa Gilda. My
heart jumped in my mouth with respect. Window boxes grew miniature Edens.
The sun some moment will stream. Break into fox-trot round table legs. My
heart feels like a host. It sticks to my roof. I take it out and put it about.
Leavened wild life everywhere. Gone-to-earth goes up the cry. I need late-night
biscuits with salt. Come see me in my urban heaven. Meet flying rats and fla-
grant saints.

It is quiet now. The apostle is still. Sweet city catnaps before sunrise. Air clean-
er and chill fresh. I watch News 24. The Americans have just bought Dawn.
Stars beyond the streetlights. I lean out my window to croon. Yes, there he is. An
unearthly hour. Ginger shock, lamp-leaning, under the manufractured moon.
G.

LATITUDES

AN ELEGY WRITTEN IN A UNMARKED NORTHERN CITY GRAVEYARD

It is.   And it is not.   A night in arms.   Long.
Flesh.   And not flesh.   Longing.
Holding high torches positioned recklessly.
From the outskirts to the inner ring.   Economic gradations.
Of colour.   Shape.   Growth.
Allocations of greenery.
The old Oak Tree.

Not just one wounded.   Drug for circulation
requiring time to intercept the breakdown with
needle point precision.
(We do not reward the lioness in action.
  We do not decorate the cunning den. Or.
  Applaud stalking.   Or.   Guerrilla tactics.)

It is still night.   It is moving.   Changing.
Still. Holly. Holly. Holly.
Evergreen.

Above.   And.   Below the crazed cracked flags the
                      inn signs swayed as is their wont in all
                      tales of ghostiness and shadowy.
                      Swayed. Wind-butted. Beaten. Thin. Hollow. Bruised emblems.
                      But here the dawn only breaks through emblems. Breaks. Yes.
                      But how! Rig dyke rising. Flying childers.
                      Ark. Angel. Apollo.
                      Dove.
                      Moonraker.
                      Yew tree.

But there are others.
The cross. of.
            Guns. Scythes. Daggers.
The anger.
The cruciform.
The rich red seepage.
Cherry Tree.

A EULOGY WRITTEN IN AN UNMARKED NORTHERN CITY PUB

It is night.   Or.   It is day.   It is timeless.
Sporadic fighting breaks.   Is quickly quelled.
All things considered.   Proximity excites.   Generating passion.
Desirability.   To have contact. To consume.   To drink deep.
Long.   Soft.   Hard.   Break and.
Soak.
Bread.

Green light from shaded pool.   Tables of time without tide.
The lilt of tower blocks with awakenings in the sky or
hibernations entrenched in basement undergrowths.
Rarely at street level.   Few wise.   Most nibble and peck.
Nuts.
Seeds.

It is see-saw-jig-saw.

                    Endless pieces. Parties of choice. And much.
                    Wet squelch littered. Concrete. Jolly kiss o' life.
                    Painted paddock. Balls. Bells. Tail backs. Feathers.
                    Dashes. Exhausts. Upside. Turnaround. Roundabout.
Let's take away.
Buttercross.
Hot fried fishes.

It is still night.   It is still day.   It is moving.   Timeless.
The traffic.
The cues.
The ebb and flow and chink of glasses.
The spills.
The queues.

All jam.   All runny.
Cherry cake.

NORTH BOUND : FACING SOUTH

Alchemical minds turn
cold boreal winters to molten
gold and
all
roads flanked with
hedgerows and horses - swish and
rush and
giddy curves of thatch.
Dumbswept.   Vibrant.   Earth-hug.

The rich nudge.

The lick of Eden.

Dangerous magic.

Still: one unbroken
flag
not to break our
necks
on would be a
treat
in this rickety
city.

Just to find
one
wild
iris.

NORTH

On this side.
A divide and cast of vowels made to swear
        to shadow the most gentle words.
Even love is flung
        gathering in the throat's pit
a stomach's empty growl.

(Don't 'luv' me cock)

The spirit roosters call and
        spread throughout the night.
Scratching dawn - morning hardly breaks.
        It ups an slithers.

The cock
s
spent up.

The hen
s
well
b
oiled.

Egg.

SOUTH BOUND : FACING NORTH

Out of tube and tune
buskers   riff
rolling would-be saints and
                    soldiers sweat.
(Stiff and prickly's the smell of it)

Such warmth is uncouth.
Such warmth leads to
        sibilants -
the thick hiss and prodding fingers
of sun and subways
                    long
        and burn for damp bronchial skies.

Listen: on the downwind
        wheezing amphibians
        full   fuff   fuff
wet-glass-hoppers
crawl and cluck
            cluck opinions
from flat and misspelt eyes
                    panning
and panting
jangled chords of
mischief dealt
fair and tenderly across its
broken bottle landscape.

            Iced
            Glint
            and
            Wink

SOUTH

The soured milk and melt of
ju-jubes sluice the jaundiced mind along
to cool shades of yesterday.

Green nostalgia.

You down hills really roll.   Smooth.
          Nubile bottoms up and falling.   Tipsy.
Your green youth and elders crawl and gang
          with prejudice.   From music to misfits.
From A to Z.

Serenade.

Gridded teeth map out.
No Entry.   Go Home.   Keep Weeping.
Keep walking that mincing
                              step
                                        right up
their street
for a short cut.
All narrowness.   All fear.

Green Sleeves.

EULOGY IN AN UNMARKED SOUTHERN COUNTY GRAVEYARD BY THE
SEA

Date to date. A hands span. That is all.
Chiselled print patterns the length of. Innings and out.
Innings and out. Weave. Tangle. Overlap.
Feet deep on a warm summers day.
Skipping tussocks. Stumbling on plots of.
The perfect way to pass
into shade
and breezy.
Kite.

Stone. Of word. Of pared image.
Of cross bones and tricorns.
A grave unsung carver.
With fingers of bone s
                    killed in
                        tra laa
                            trilling
                                calligraphy.

Skeletal craft. Skimming. Sea lap.
Harbour lips. Rictus. Kiss.
Sucks slowly.
Sucks.
Gulls.

Growth gang. Ging and. Blue chipped. Marble.
Date to date. A hands span. A spirit cheer. Clinks.
Let's fly.
Lark.

Rich one. Poor one. Beggar both. The
opposition to life is
massive and sustained.
Innings and out.
Clock.
Tock.
Cuckoo.

So this is England.   Blanched.   Steeped.
Mouths full of marbles and scratchings.
Speeches full of leftovers.   Full of fag ends.   Full of slops.
Served with a face that gives
medicine a lift and
a leg up to
merriment.
Carnival.
Cock.
Chafer.

The snug.   The warm sickly draught.   Of insularity.
Stagnation.   Exclusion.   Pick yer winda.
                  Pick any
                             thing
                                    to throw and smash the
                                    winged and
                                    wounded.
                                    Dragon.
                                    Fly.

Some union Jack.   Some bloody union.   Remember Jack.
Flying flags. Pigs might, Flies might. Fists might,
No Jack.   Not pickets Jack.   Don't talk wet.   Don't talk
soft Jack.
Jenny.
Wren.
Cherry.
Cake.
Runny.
Oak.
Cricket.

OPUS ANGLICANUM—

(movement)

taunts sewn daily
beaming
a cluster
of ad-ages: history   history   history
will be sore-winged with
selective forgiving

A cast shedding envy
throughout Europe. oui ya sí
we gave them
a-needling to die for
couching ore sprigs
into brand ancient chasubles of awe
so much so they named it after us
        O-Opus Anglicanum
'England is for us surely a garden
of delights - an inexhaustible well' -
so sang Papa Innocent to our choral copes
and mitres.

what beauty we unravelled

(movement)
With every fibre of spin
Ministers of Misrule
thread-paint moral empires on their
sleeves. pink pink pink
go the shears at the wrists
on the edge of the wood

secular embroidery
- what stands still long enough -
catches trappings
banners palls purses
underneath and hidden linen
outre vestments
couched bed hangings
misleading cushions
runners
lips lying in wait
you name it
       O
     Opus!
and a pair of shin-new
leg-long buskins found
in a power-tomb in Canterbury
where a cathedral is

still

a metre of petersham
will
stiff out a great coat
with
sham to spare for
fair war

just

(movement)

stuckup on thorn hedge
hemmed in
broderie anglaise
capped
pearlies kink the may day
blossom floss
a fly pass is
buzzing her maj
at enormous expense
the sky streaks red white
blue
on blue

Intelligence born in sour light
cramps eyes guiding the gilt ~
a sequence of sequins
is a chain of glitzer
on the slope
going blind for an
            anthem is a song
                      too high
on a hot bright morning in
a strained voice
he sang
across the waters:

'we have not yet found shiny
pointy things we call weapons'

expert
embroiderers
finger their bodkins
weaving empires

upon time

threads get knotted

Dong! The history drowns.

PA(X)

Many centralisations
               across the universe:
Andromeda in a spin.
Nether Edge slippin
dow
n its
o
  w
     n
*h*il
    l
s*k*
i
n.
The virgin statue leaking
           weeps in
               Venezuela.
The corner shop.
A dark bar.
Some field.
Every bus stop.
Texas over
a barrel.
Burma in the
doldrums.
      Ang Sang Sui as ever under house arrest:
Flowers
    hang fire
        in her o-so tired hair.

inherhair

             ~

Bloodsuch
                eye of Mars
ahems
                on Earth -
after weeks of clear skies
clouds
            perverse
beneath
blocked horizons of contempt -
as if *we* care -
eye-poking
teeth-extroothing
amputations
is an ongoing
gong-gifter
a swash of derring-do
so be gone
mythical mads &
planetary charismatics
            -   yo   -
          - love   -
        don't live here
            anymore

~

Sidereal time emphasizes
reversed profiles:
(or so it says on the back of
my imaginary pack of cards)
pink lint and gauze
re-verse in-verse
draw a load of
pesterers along the rind
of raw.

Is it too late
or too early
in worldstory
to talk seriously
about
ticky emotions?

Try this:

Dark strutters lept icebreakers.
Happy-sads skim purring hurt.
A-leapt-frogging all intellect leaves
outstanding orders to wilt-out
the bleeding heart
Bbbbbbbbbbbbbbbbbbbbbbbbbbbb
bbbbbbbblllllllllllllleeeeeeeeeeeeeeeeedddddddddssssssss

Let's amend August :
bicker-out invasion planning
drift-ift to September
without maim

It's a start.

O

It's an

A

80

SHED

What seeps in 'n' out of knot-holes?
…………..w..h..i..s..p..s……….
Inaudible messages from outer
trumpetings
          cranny insects
money-spiders
          dosh-dosh
nut carpings
squirrel proof frustrations
          detached eyeballs
                    o' spoowks
louche fingers
     stiffening
draughts
positions of light imitating
                    blonde eyelashes
          an unblink
murder of
          imagined bird
                    beak
   of
    of
     of luna beam at double noon
shoot out
              the unseasoned bleed of
       resin
a variety of stigmatas
                    invisible
pollutants too dangerous
to list
          the name of the day
                    better not dwelt on.

Block them up.

Close the perpex windows.

500 tonnes equals
bio-hazard sludge-upping
North Sea gizzard
casting
wholesides
of our Isles
darker
than
shark-shadow
stealth
contaminating
night-scented
stocks
l i s t i n g l i s t i n g
arthritic
ghost ships
denser that
woder
    water
       watter
non-solvable
mercy-all
lead
mercury
chromium
cadmium
asbestos
spumed peeling
painted throat

heading for Mandyland.

Shut that door!

Perspex is not the
incomparable sashay of bombé glass

Do not stay still in front of her curves

The diamond slasht
                    light
trussed at angles
            coming at you
at all ways
            side-jaw'd
in a shudder of
                absinthe
a twist of
                eau-de-nil
and f-fake prophesy

Do not stay still in front of her curves

promenade the
long room of
Haddon Hall -
do it with hands on hips -
gavotte it! ~!~~!~time

travel

the 21st century is ill
at ease
the Euphrates
in conflict
runs out of sorts
thinning to
thinner than
lavender water
and f-fake prophesy

Find seed tray:

sow n grow a perfect wall.

If we rid the world
of territorial
desire would
it
bang to rights—
would I
would I
share my shed?

'It was war we weren't blowing kisses'

Not much shelter
in those words
for the limping
armless
              lipless
and gang-got.

Wooden walls
flim-timbre
          tinder
                cinder

Perspex windows
self-scratch
in the night.

The door lock is not
pickproof.

The alarm bells unbought.

It is no place to hide
from civil conflict

high minded winds

f-fake memories

OTHER TITLES FROM AHADADA

Ahadada Books publishes poetry. Preserving the best of the small press tradition, we produce finely designed and crafted books in limited editions.

the time at the end of this writing (Paolo Javier)   0-9732233-2-4
"These are perceptive poems; that there is pleasure despite it all in never knowing what might happen next is no small part of what they know. "
          —Anselm Berrigan, author of *Integrity and Dramatic Life*

Investigations (Márton Koppány)   0-9732233-1-6
"Of the minimalists who have sought wider accessibility through their work, few have done as well as Koppány."
          —Karl Young, *The Light & Dust Anthology of Poetry*

Strange Currencies (Daniel Sendecki)   0-9732233-0-8
"Among our elements, where the human situation locates the self as always on tour, via poetry, here, epistles of transformative myth."
          —Michael Basinski

Song To Arepo (Jesse Glass)   3-89810-184-3
"His rhythms are vigorous, his imagery is strong and inventive; and his language has, in places, a burly force that reminds me of Geoffrey Hill."
          —Jane Somerville, *The American Book Review*

The Book of Doll (Jesse Glass)   3-89810-185-1
"Glass´s work has a strong narrative style which leads the reader (or auditor) through glittering images and strange, speculative environments."
          —Karl Young, *The Shepherd Express*

www.ahadadabooks.com